# WALKING C__

# EYE BROOK near UPPINGHAM

Number Nine in the popular series of walking guides

## Contents

| Walk | | Miles | Page No |
|---|---|---|---|
| 1 | Blaston Hollows | 7 | 4 |
| 2 | Eyebrook Reservoir | 5 | 6 |
| 3 | Stoke Dry Wood | 6 | 8 |
| 4 | Hare Pie Bank | 7 | 10 |
| 5 | Nevill Holt | 7½ | 12 |
| 6 | Wardley Hill | 5¾ | 14 |
| 7 | Crackbottle | 7 | 16 |
| 8 | Not Quite to Lyddington | 6½ | 18 |
| 9 | Allexton Park | 7½ | 20 |

Walked, Written and Drawn by Clive Brown
© Clive Brown 2002
2nd Edition © Clive Brown 2008 – 2011

Published by Clive Brown
ISBN 978-1-907669-09-5

# PLEASE
## Take care of the countryside
## Your leisure is someone's livelihood

Close gates
Start no fires
Keep away from livestock and animals
Do not stray from marked paths
Take litter home
Do not damage walls, hedgerows or fences
Cross only at stiles or gates
Protect plants, trees and wildlife
Keep dogs on leads
Respect crops, machinery and rural property
Do not contaminate water

Although not essential we recommend good walking boots; during hot weather take something to drink on the way. All walks can easily be negotiated by an averagely fit person. The routes have been recently walked and surveyed, changes can however occur, please follow any signed diversions. Some paths cross fields which are under cultivation. All distances and times are approximate.

The maps give an accurate portrayal of the area, but scale has however been sacrificed in some cases for the sake of clarity and to fit restrictions of page size.

Walking Close To have taken every care in the research and production of this guide but cannot be held responsible for the safety of anyone using them.

During very wet weather, parts of these walks may become impassable through flooding, check before starting out. Stiles and rights of way can get overgrown during the summer; folding secateurs are a useful addition to a walker's rucksack.

Thanks to Angela for help in production of these booklets

Views or comments?
walkingcloseto@yahoo.co.uk

Reproduced from Ordnance Survey Mapping on behalf of The Controller of Her Majesty's Stationery Office. © Crown Copyright License No. 100037980.

# Walking Close to Eye Brook near Uppingham

Uppingham, situated at the junction of the A47 and the A6003, halfway between Leicester and Peterborough, reflects its modest size with the fact that it is the second town of Rutland, England's smallest county. It is a charming mixture of redbrick and stone with little modern development. The town dates from the early middle ages. It received its charter for a weekly market in 1281 from King Edward I. The school, founded in 1584 by Archdeacon Robert Johnson, still uses its original building behind the church as part of its extensive campus.

Eye Brook rises close to the village of Tilton on the Hill and wriggles its way to the Welland close to Corby, never very full or fast flowing. It marks the border between Leicestershire and Rutland for much of the way before going through Eyebrook Reservoir.

Lyddington, mentioned in the Domesday Book, has many impressive and attractive 17$^{th}$ and 18$^{th}$ century ironstone buildings. The Bede House was originally part of the medieval Palace for the bishop of Lincoln. It was confiscated at the reformation and given to the Cecil family; Thomas Cecil, in 1600 had the building converted to an almshouse. The residents of this establishment were required to say prayers for him and all subsequent Earls and Marquises of Exeter. The house continued to be used for this purpose until 1930; it is now an English Heritage property.

Stoke Dry dates from the 11$^{th}$ century. Sir Everard Digby 1578-1606, part of the Digby family local to Stoke Dry, converted to Catholicism and was executed after being implicated in the gunpowder plot.

The Little Owl, not a native species, was first introduced into this country as a household pet during the 19th Century. It was found to be useful for catching cockroaches. By the 1890's they were breeding locally and can be seen in the local countryside. Only the size of a song thrush, it hunts during the day as well as the night, chiefly for insects, worms and small mammals. It will also take small birds during the nesting season.

Rutland and Leicestershire have made walking within their boundaries considerably easier with the widespread use of yellow topped marker posts; keep a watchful eye for these during your walks.

We feel that it would be difficult to get lost with the instructions and map in this booklet, but recommend carrying an Ordnance Survey map. All walks are on Explorer Map Nos. 224, 233 and 234; Landranger No. 141 covers at a smaller scale. Roads, geographical features and buildings, not on our map but visible from the walk can be easily identified.

# 1   Blaston Hollows

## 7 Miles              $3^1/_2$ Hours

Park in Hallaton village, no toilets, two local pubs the Bewicke Arms and the Fox Inn.  This walk will be muddy in wet weather.  Avoid Easter Monday.

**1**   Start from the eastern side of North End, signposted Horninghold.  Bear left down a tarmac driveway as the road forks right.  Go through the farmyard and over stiles each end of a short enclosed path and maintain direction to the bottom corner of the field ahead.  Cross the stiles either side of the disused railway.

**2**   The field ahead may be under cultivation but the track should be visible through any crop.  Cross straight over to the yellow topped post on the other side.  Carry on over the footbridge and follow the arrowed direction on the marker post; this field may also have a crop in it, if there is no apparent track, bear right just before the flat summit of the hill and cross to the yellow topped post visible in the hedge in the direction of Horninghold village.  Cross the stile/footbridge and the narrow neck of field.  Continue over the footbridge and the next field (a track should be visible) to the farm buildings at the top left of the field; go through the gate.

**3**   Turn right down this tarmac farm road to the village and left in front of the church.  Carry on out of the village and fork left at the junction.  As Horninghold Wood on the right ends, turn right and follow the edge of the field with the wood to the right.

**4**   At the corner of the field bear right through the gate, turn left to the corner of the hedge that juts out and then keep original direction.  Walk on, with the hedge to the left and parallel with the telegraph poles, to the bottleneck at the end.  Go through the gate, bear right down a short track and turn left before the next gate.  Continue over the stile, into the parkland and past the front of Stockerston Hall.  Turn left through a small handgate next to a double metal gate and turn right.

**5**   After 200yds turn right over a stile into the field just vacated, follow the arrowed direction across two stiles.  Keep going up the hill, heading to the left of the trees on the right.  Cross a stile and carry straight on over this next field primarily 30yds away and parallel to Bolt Wood on the right.  Continue over the dyke by the marker post and another stile.  Go up to the corner past the Ordnance Survey pillar and cross the next stile by Stockerston crossroads.

**6**   Turn right, walk 600yds to a signpost and turn left along the field edge.  Keep direction along this bridleway past gates, with Highland Spinney and the hedge to the left.  Continue past the marker post into the corner and turn right, with Blaston Hollows to the left walk into the next corner turn right again.  Follow the track round

**Completed on the next Page (Six)**

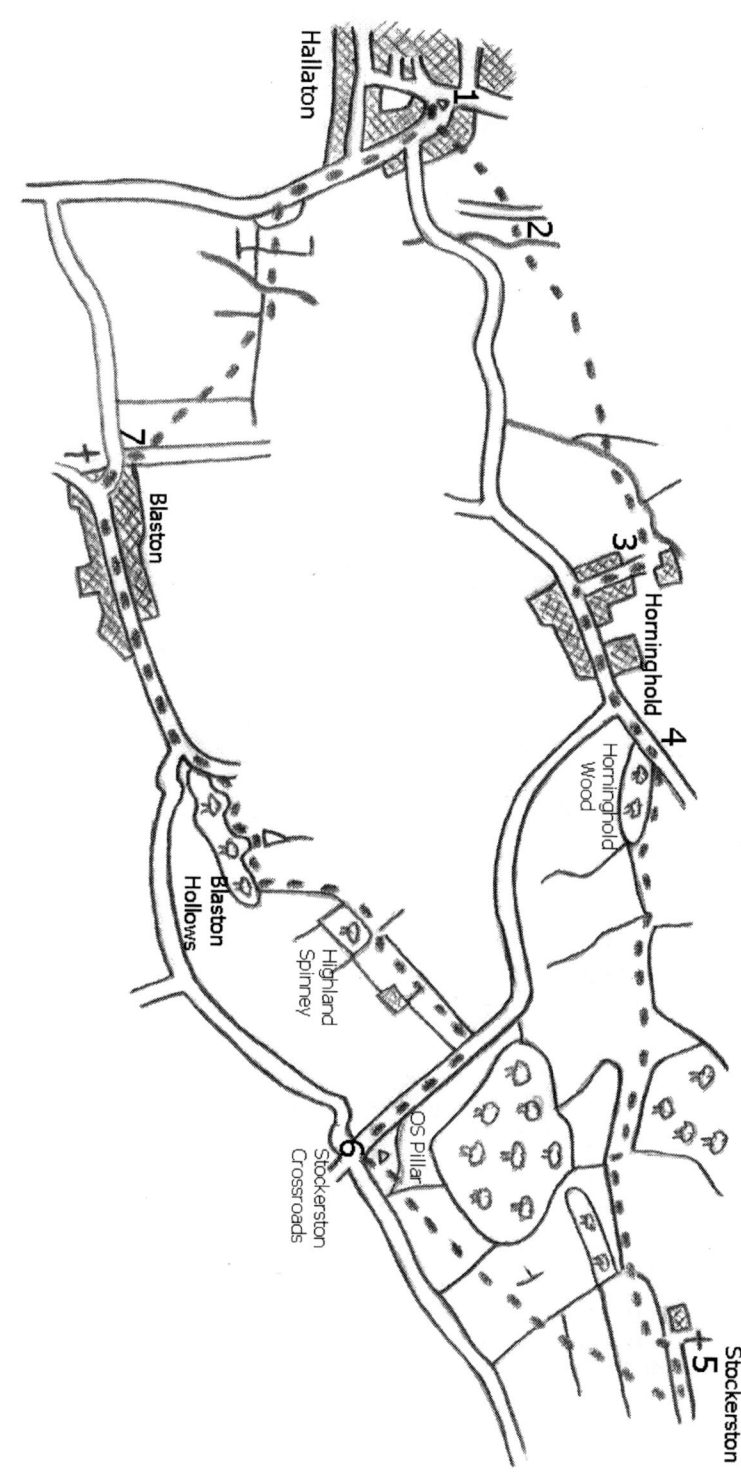

**Completion of 1 Blaston Hollows from the previous Page**

to the left through the gap and keep along the field edge with Blaston Hollows to the left. Join the farm road to the left, carry straight on down the road into Blaston village to the junction and turn right.

**7** Go straight on at the corner through the metal gates ahead, bear left at the marker post and take a diagonal left to a stile just out of sight on the left. Cross the next field in the direction of the arrow to the bottom right corner, go over the footbridge and through the gap in the hedge. Turn left; follow the edge of the field to a gate and cross the stream. Maintain direction over this field and two more marked stiles; go through the gate to the road and turn right. This road leads directly into Hallaton and your vehicle.

# 2  Eyebrook Reservoir

5 Miles                      2½ Hours

Park in the space at the corner of the road to the west of Stoke Dry village next to the reservoir. No toilets, no refreshments.

**1** Turn right out of the parking area, walk up the hill through the village and bear right to the crossroads at the A6003.

**2** Cross the stile opposite and follow the track diagonally over the field more or less parallel with the telegraph poles, the yellow top of the marker post next to the gate can be seen above the hedge. This field may be under cultivation but the track should be visible through any crop. Maintain the direction of the marker arrow from the gate across the next two fields. Cross the double stile/footbridge and continue over the hill towards Lyddington church ahead; the next yellow top post will come into view. Join the road after the stile in the top corner of the next field.

**3** Turn left, walk up to the Main street and turn right, follow the road out of the village to the derestriction signs and turn right at the stile just beyond. Go over the field and the next stile and through the farmyard.

**4** Continue over the stile and up to the far corner of this field, cross the footbridge and turn right along the edge of the field to the next stile. Step over and walk diagonally left to the top left corner, the track should be visible even if there is a crop in the field. Carry on over the narrow corner of a field and a stile; turn left a short way along the field edge and turn left over the stile footbridge at the marker. Take a right hand diagonal over this field, cross a stile and walk over the ridged field to the stile by the pumping station ahead. Go down the short piece of roadway and cross the busy A6003.

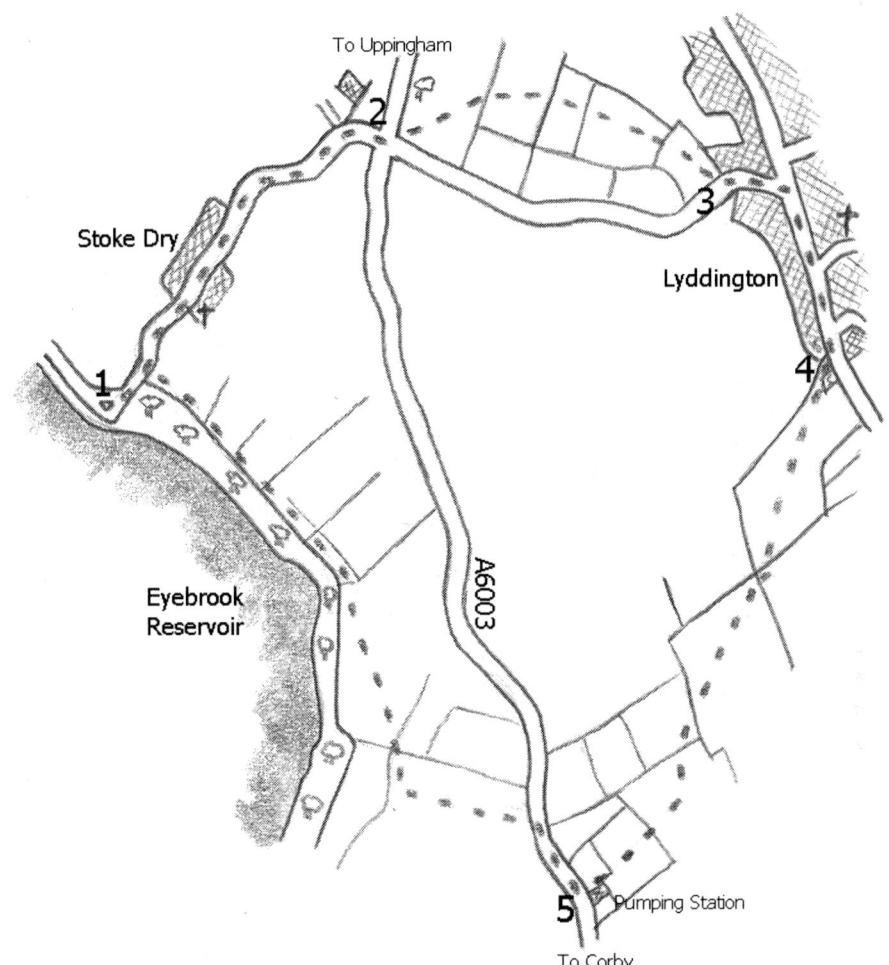

**5** Turn right and follow the wide grass verge to the next bridleway sign to the left at the top of a slight rise.  Go up the slope following the obvious path between fields.  Turn right to the corner, cross a farm road with marker posts either side and carry on diagonally to the opposite corner of this field down a normally well marked path.  Continue through the gate along the green bridleway between hedges; go through another gate and maintain this direction along field edges and through gates to the road between the reservoir and Stoke Dry.  Turn left and walk down to your vehicle.

**Eyebrook Reservoir,** started in June 1936, was completed in late 1939.  The 'Dambusters' team practised here before their operation over Germany.  It is now an important wildlife conservation area.

# 3    Stoke Dry Wood

### 6 Miles            3 Hours

Park in either of the free car parks off North Street East close to the centre of Uppingham.  Toilets, restaurants, cafes, shops and pubs in the town 100 to 200yds.

**1**   Leave the car park to the left and walk towards the traffic lights.  Go through Hope's Yard to the left, turn left along High Street East and then right into Queen Street.  Carry on past the library and turn right then left almost immediately down the signposted footpath.  Cross the stile over the iron fence and the footbridge, continue up the hill at a slight diagonal and over the next stile.  Walk along the right hand side of the field past the yellow topped post and through the scrubland.

**2**   Turn to the left down the farm road and right not much further on at the signpost, continue over four stiles to the bottom of the dip and up the other side.  Turn left after the stile at the top, look out for the marker post on the left and turn to the right, this is across a football pitch so please make a detour if a game is in progress.  Go through the hedge gap and over the stile half hidden to the left.  Carry on diagonally left to the corner of the field and on to the road.

**3**   Cross the stile on the other side of the road and go diagonally left, a yellow topped post will come into view once the hill has been crested.  Maintain direction through two fields over footbridges marked by yellow top posts, walk into the far corner of the third field and onto the road.

**4**   Carry on over the stile on the other side of the road, bear slightly right and follow the arrow marker over the double stile.  Continue direction over several stiles well marked by yellow topped posts to a footpath sign and turn right.  Walk down the enclosed green bridleway to Main Street in Lyddington and turn left.

**5**   Go up to the village centre and turn right at the road signposted Stoke Dry.  After 200yds turn right over a stile and follow the arrowed direction over the field, cross the stile and continue up and over the hill.  Cross two more stiles and go through a gate; these fields may be under cultivation but a track should be visible through them.  Turn diagonally left and walk to the opposite corner, parallel to, but about 10yds away from the telegraph poles.

**6**   Cross the busy A6003 and carry on along the road opposite, after 300yds turn right at the signpost through the high metal gate.  Carry on through the wooden gate and along the left hand side of the field; continue through another gate and the left hand side of a narrow field.  After this next gate go around the right hand edge of the field and through the gate and straight on at the second marker post.  Follow this bridleway with the hedge to the right to Stoke Dry Wood.

**7** Turn right and follow the path keeping the edge of the wood to the left, as the wood ends keep going along the gravel path to the road and turn left. As the road turns to the left go over the stile to the right.

**8** Continue over the next stile along the right hand side of the field to a marker post. Cross the stile and the field beyond at a slight angle to a gap in the hedge marked by a yellow top post, the path should be visible through any crop. Follow the fenced track and cross a very narrow bridge and stile. Maintain direction over the corner of the next field, and then several more fields well marked with the ever present yellow topped posts; join the road to the left into the centre of Uppingham and your vehicle.

# 4 Hare Pie Bank

### 7 Miles  3$^{1}/_{2}$ Hours

Park in Hallaton village, no toilets, two local pubs the Bewicke Arms and the Fox Inn. This walk will be muddy in wet weather. Avoid Easter Monday.

**1** Start from the church, walk down churchgate on the north side of the church, bear right past the school and follow the road round to a yellow topped marker post. Go through a kissing gate and along the left hand side of the field signposted Cranoe. Carry on through the gate, when the hedge stops cross over to the stile.

**2** Turn left after the stile/footbridge, follow the left hand edge of the fields over the low wire fence, bear right with the field edge and turn left over a double stile.

**3** The open field ahead may be under cultivation but the track should be visible through any crop. Cross the field in the arrowed direction just to the right of the rectangular pond, walk through the hedge between posts and over the next field to the yellow top post visible in front of the wood. Continue through Horseclose Spinney on an obvious track, go over the bridge and maintain direction over the next field, the track should be well marked through any crop.

**4** Go between the farm buildings with the brick one to the left, turn left then right at the end between the hedge and the barn. Carry on through the gate along the right hand edge of the field and the double metal gate. Bear slightly right over the field parallel to but 30yds away from the hedge on the right. Go through the hedge gap and keep going over the stile and through the dip to the road.

**5** Turn left past the edge of the village of Cranoe and straight over the crossroads, to a signpost just around the slight left hand bend; turn left through the gates.

**6** Walk down the left hand side of the field go through the gate and turn right. Continue along this well waymarked path, with the dyke on the right, to the road. Cross and carry on next to the dyke over two fields and between disused bridge piers to the next road; turn left.

**7** Walk along the road past the railway and up the hill to the crossroads. Take the potholed bridleway ahead signposted Field Road Hallaton. Continue to the road and turn left, walk 100yds and turn right through the gate and down the right hand side of the next two fields. Cross into the enclosed bridleway and go up the slope, nearly to the top of Hare Pie Hill/Bank to a marker post.

**8** Turn right, cross the field and go down the slope with the trees to the left past the marker post, continue over the stile/footbridge and up the enclosed footpath through the archway into Hallaton and your vehicle.

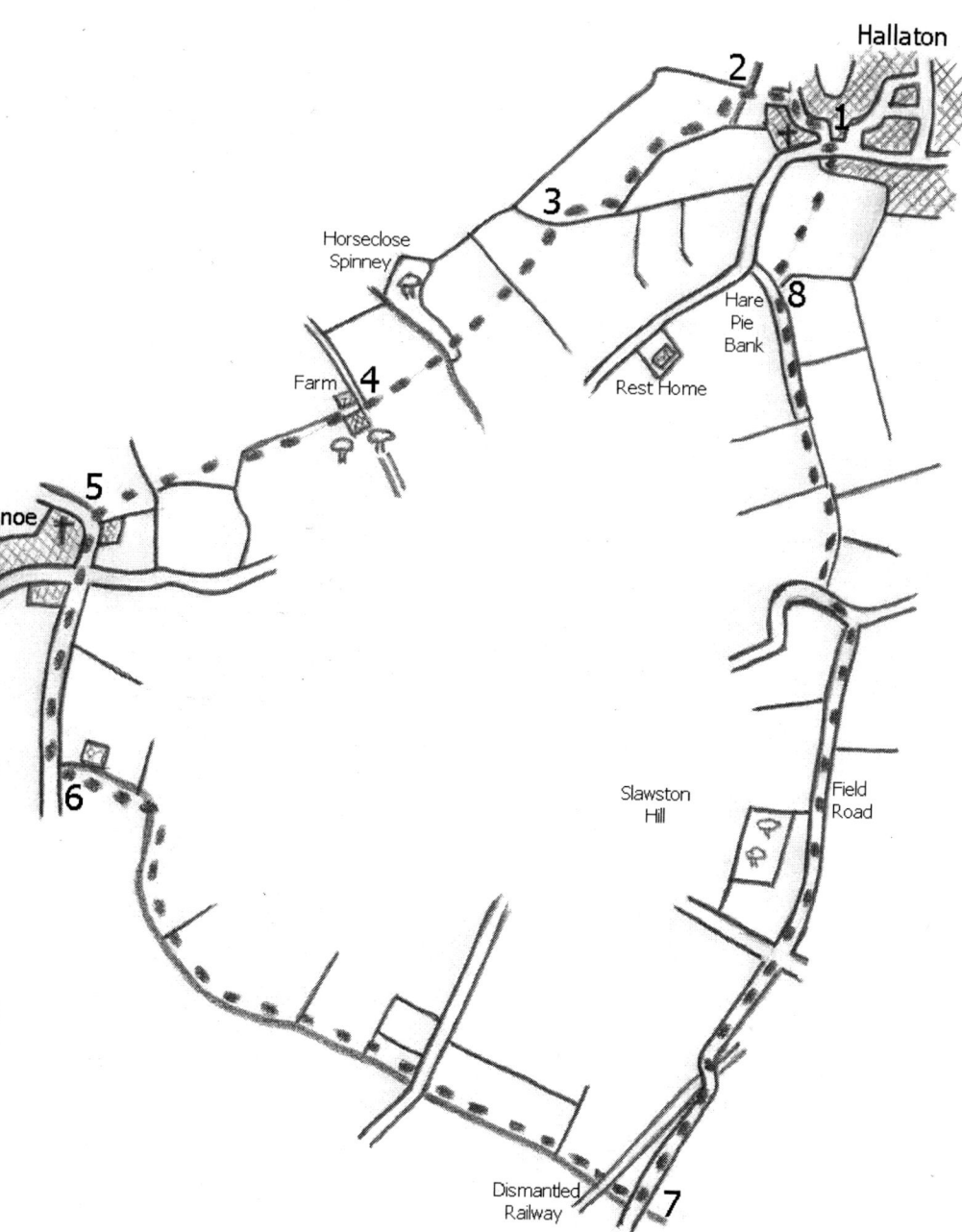

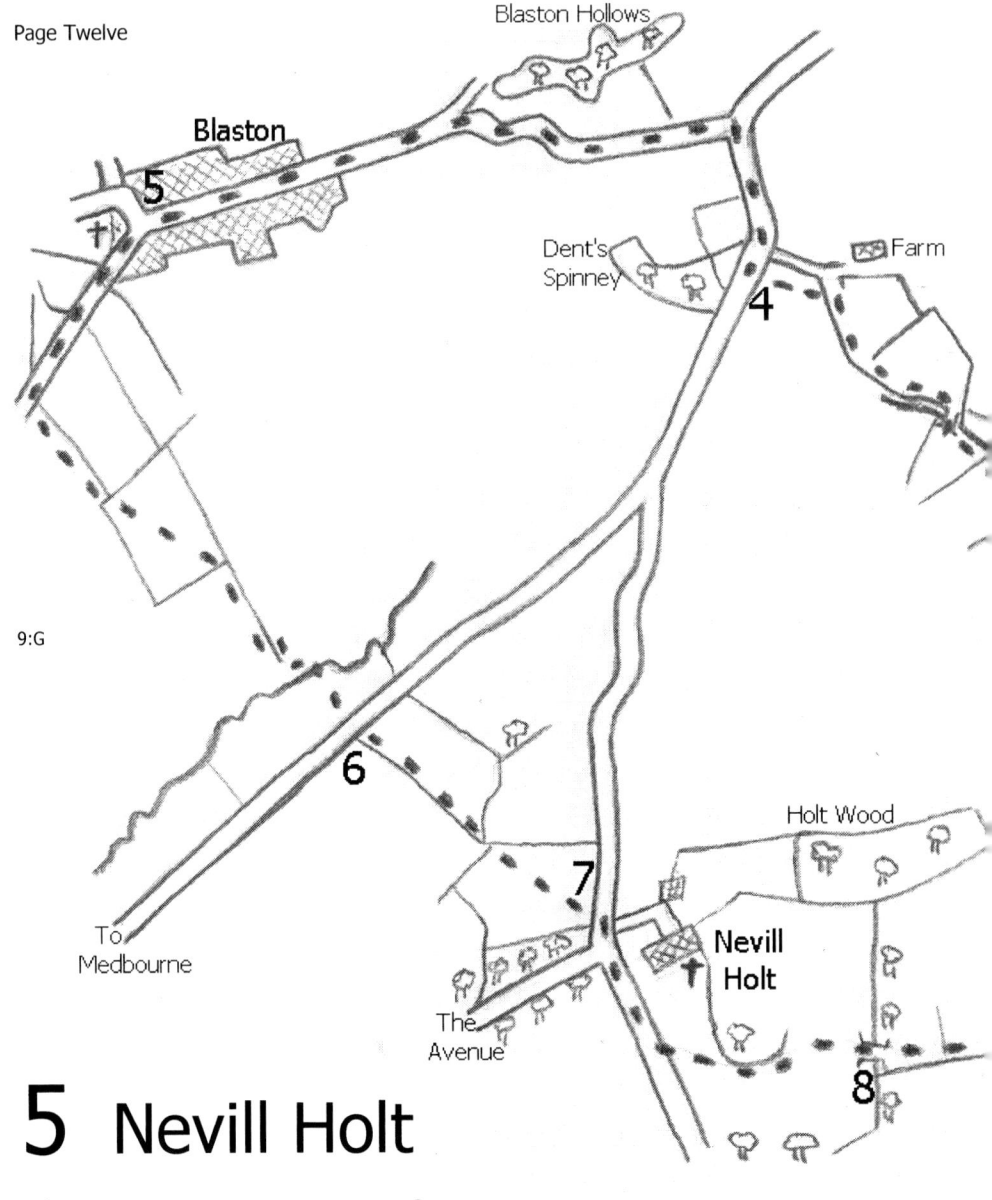

# 5 Nevill Holt

7$^{1}/_{2}$ Miles      3$^{3}/_{4}$ Hours

Park in Great Easton, no toilets, local shop and pub 'The Sun'.

**1**  Walk north out of the village on Stockerston Lane.  Turn left at the footpath sign for Blaston and immediate right between hedges.  Cross the stile at the end and the next double stile ahead.  Keep noting yellow topped marker posts and take a left diagonal across the field, past a hedge corner and follow the edge of the field, the hedge to the right. Step over this stile and take a left diagonal again, climb over the fence onto Holt Lane, a green bridleway.

**2** Walk 40yds to the left, go to the right through the metal gate and get back to the diagonal direction to the left. Continue over the next stile bearing slightly right; maintain direction through a gate and over a stile/footbridge. Cross the corner of the next field which may be under cultivation although the track should be marked.

**3** Turn right and follow the path between the stream to the left and the field to the right. 150yds after the second stile turn left over a substantial sleeper bridge. Turn right, back to the original direction along the opposite bank. Cross a stile and then go straight across the bottom of the next field. Continue on the right hand side of this new field next to the stream; towards the end, before the telegraph poles are reached, turn right over a footbridge and then left to keep direction. Go through a boundary and up to the corner of this field; turn left over a stile, opposite the marker post and go to the right, around the edge of this field to the road.

**4** Turn to the right, walk down the road to the junction and turn left. Continue to the junction close to the church in Blaston, signposted Medbourne and turn left.

**5** Follow this field road uphill to a bridleway signposted left, walk up the slope with the hedge to the left and through the gate at the top. Cross the next field to the bottom left corner, the track should be visible through any crop. Go through the hedge gap and continue down the left hand side of the field, turn left through the gateway nearly at the bottom. Walk to the right around the end of the field and turn right through the hedge gap before the woodland juts out. Go over the field, the path should be seen within the crop, to the gate.

**Completed on the next Page (Fourteen)**

Page Thirteen

## Completion of 5 Nevill Holt from the previous Page

**6** Cross the road and keep direction uphill on the right hand side of the left hand field, continue through the gate at the top and over the field to the left of the first telegraph pole.

**7** Go down the road to the right, straight on at the junction past Nevill Holt School. Turn left at the second metal gate at the bridleway sign, cross to the marker post and bear right with the trees to the left. Carry straight on past two marker posts (follow the blue arrows) to a yellow top marker post and go through gates either side of a bridge over a narrow stream.

**8** Cross this field to the top right corner go through a gate and down the right hand side of the field. Turn right through the second metal gate and cross diagonally to the opposite corner. Continue through a large and a small gate and along the left hand side of two fields to join the stream coming in from the left. Go left through the hedge gap and follow the course of the stream keeping it to the left. Eventually the stream veers left and the path goes past two metal gates to a yellow top marker post next to a smaller gate.

**9** Turn left through a short enclosed path over the stream and right after the next gate. Follow the track with the stream on the right, go through the gate and turn left to walk into the village and find your vehicle.

# 6 Wardley Hill

### $5^3/_4$ Miles $\qquad$ $2^3/_4$ Hours

**Park in the lay-by** on the north side of the A47, 300yds east of the junction for Allexton and Belton in Rutland, at the bottom of Wardley Hill, 3 miles west of Uppingham. No toilets, caravan café open early morning to early afternoon, pubs in Belton.

**1** Find the signpost on the north side of the lay-by and go through the gate beyond. Take the grass path ahead between fields to the crossroads of paths and keep direction through the hedge gap. Carry on ahead along the right hand side of the field with the hedge on the right, up and over the hill. At the T-junction at the bottom, turn right.

**2** As another track joins from the left turn right along it for 40yds and then follow the track to the left. Carry on past the T-junction to the field corner, bear left, then right just before the trees and continue up the hill.

**3** At the top, turn right and almost double back along the crest of the ridge with the hedge to the left and keep going all the way to the A47.

**4** Cross carefully and turn left, (it may be possible to use the old piece of road here), continue to the junction for Uppingham and turn right.

**5** Walk 60yds to the signpost and turn right trough the gate and along the obvious track about 100yds from the left hand field edge. Carry on through the next field getting closer to the left hand edge and into the corner of the field. Maintain direction across the next two fields; go through the gate and into Wardley Wood.

**6** Carry on to a junction of paths close to the centre of the wood; be very careful here. Walk diagonally left along a grass path which is well marked by yellow arrows; do not go straight on along the hardcore path.

**7** At the end of the wood, turn right down the gravel path and follow as it turns right with the hedge to the left; carry on as it meanders between fields into Wardley village. Turn left at the church and walk up to the A47.

**8** Cross and continue down the tree lined bridleway. Bear left along the old A47 for 40yds and then turn right through the hedge gap; go over the stile and follow the arrowed direction through the dip, over the sleeper bridge and the next stile on the upslope. Continue down the left hand side of the field to the marker post, turn left and cross the field along the outward path. Go through the hedge gate to the lay-by and your vehicle.

Page Fifteen

# 7 Crackbottle

### 7 Miles      3$^{1}/_{2}$ Hours

Park in Hallaton village, no toilets, two local pubs the 'Bewicke Arms' and the 'Fox Inn'. This walk will be muddy in wet weather. Avoid Easter Monday.

**1** Walk north out of the village towards East Norton, at the fork in the road go straight on over the stile. Take a diagonal to the right. There may be a crop in this field but there should be an obvious path through it, if not head towards a bridge half hidden in the line of trees. Continue over the corner of the next field and over the old railway bridge.

**2** From the foot of the bridge, cross the field ahead on a right hand diagonal, the track again should be obvious through any crop. Bear right level with the marker post on the right and continue ahead over the footbridge and the next field. Cross the double stile and maintain direction uphill, with the hedge to the left, through the gate at the top. Cross the next stile and go through two gates.

**3** Turn left along the hardcore bridleway; continue through the small gate and down the right hand side of the field. Bear left in the corner, walk past the Ordnance Survey triangulation pillar to the next corner. Cross the stile and keep direction now along the edge of the field, on to the hardcore bridleway, over the disused railway tunnel and eventually to the road.

**4** Turn right for 200yds, as the road starts to bear right, go left through a gate at a signpost. Follow the edge of the field with the wood to the right. Turn left, then right, then left again round the corner. Go halfway down the slope; turn right through a gate, then left back to the original direction alongside Crackbottle Spinney. Walk down the slope 100yds and turn left through the gate and the trees, then right to rejoin the original field edge. Carry on down to Crackbottle Road.

**5** Walk along the road to the right and keep going to the T-junction for Tugby. Turn left down the farm road opposite, signposted Midshires Way. Fork left at the marker post and follow the concrete road through the farm and up the gentle rise. Go through the gate and onward between hedge and fence. As the bridleway turns right by the marker post, go straight on over the field, which may be under cultivation. Continue over a cattle grid, across a field, through a gateway (the woods either side are called Hallaton Spinneys) and down the farm road beyond.

**6** At the next gateway and marker post turn right, go through a gate at the corner of the wood, Moor Hill Spinneys, and follow the left hand edge of the field uphill. Cross a narrow piece of field and carry on down the left hand side of the next field. Keep direction through a gate and along the edges of the next three fields.

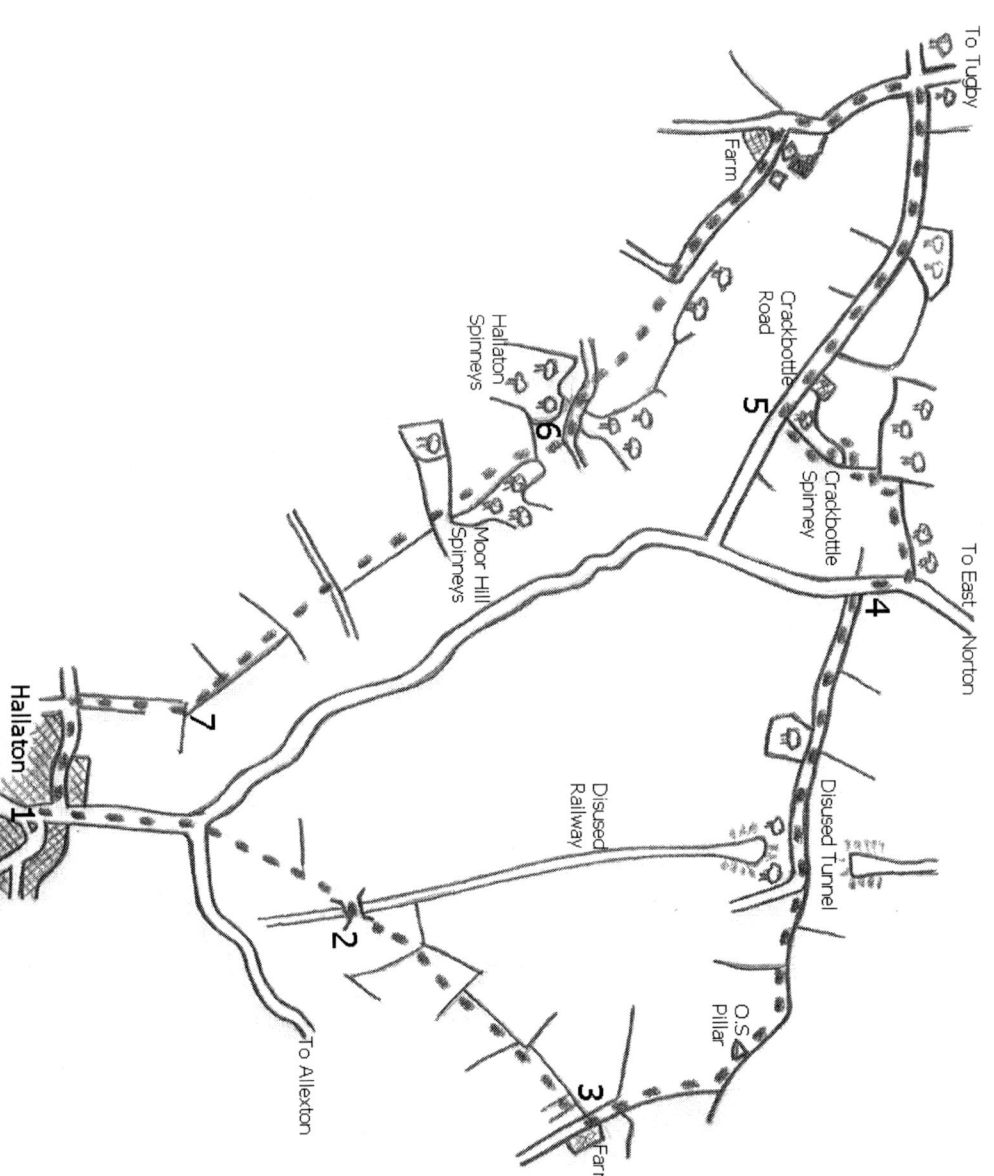

**7** At the next gate, go through, turn right and follow the field edge with the hedge to the right. Continue through the gate and down the enclosed path to the road. Turn left back into Hallaton and your vehicle.

9:G

# 8  Not Quite to Lyddington

## 6½ Miles     3 Hours

Park in either of the free car parks off North Street East, close to the centre of Uppingham. Toilets, restaurants, cafes, shops and pubs in the town 100 to 200yds.

**1**  Turn right out of the car park along North Street East and Glaston Road; fork right opposite the railings on the left. Continue as the road bears right and between fields as the hedges stop. Go past the yellow top marker post, down the tree and hedge lined path into Bisbrooke village.

**2**  Bear right at the end of the track and left at the T-junction. Go down the road to the right, marked church only, at the phone box. Carry on past the church down the green bridleway; maintain direction downhill and cross a stile. Go over the field ahead in the arrowed direction and over the next stile by a marker post. Cross the rickety footbridge and go on to the next stile in the far corner.

**3**  Cross the old railway line, turn left then right around the field edge. At the corner carry straight on over the field, which may be under cultivation but the track should be visible. Maintain direction on the path between the fields, cross a stile and the next field to the road, in Seaton village.

**4**  Turn right; approaching the end of the village bear left into Grange Lane. Continue past the farm; go over two stiles and along the right hand edge of the field with the stream to the right. Bear left away from the stream at a marker post with a dyke now to the right; at the next marker post turn right for a short distance before turning left almost immediately, now with a hedge on the right. Cross a stile and continue between trees and hedge, go over the next stile and turn immediate right over another stile (not straight on into Lyddington).

**5**  Maintain direction now over a series of narrow fields and well marked stiles, to the road. Cross the road and the stile on the opposite right; take a right diagonal uphill over three well marked stiles. Go over the next field through which a track should be visible, cross the road and the stile opposite.

**6**  Follow the arrowed direction over the field to the marker post, walk across the playing field and turn left then right at marker posts. Carry on down the dip and up the other side, turn left at the signpost, walk 100yds and turn right at another signpost. Maintain direction over fields and the footbridge to the road in Uppingham (Southview). Turn right and then left into Queen Street, walk past the 'Cross Keys', turn left into High Street East and right into the passageway called Hope's Yard. Turn right along North Street East to the car park and your vehicle.

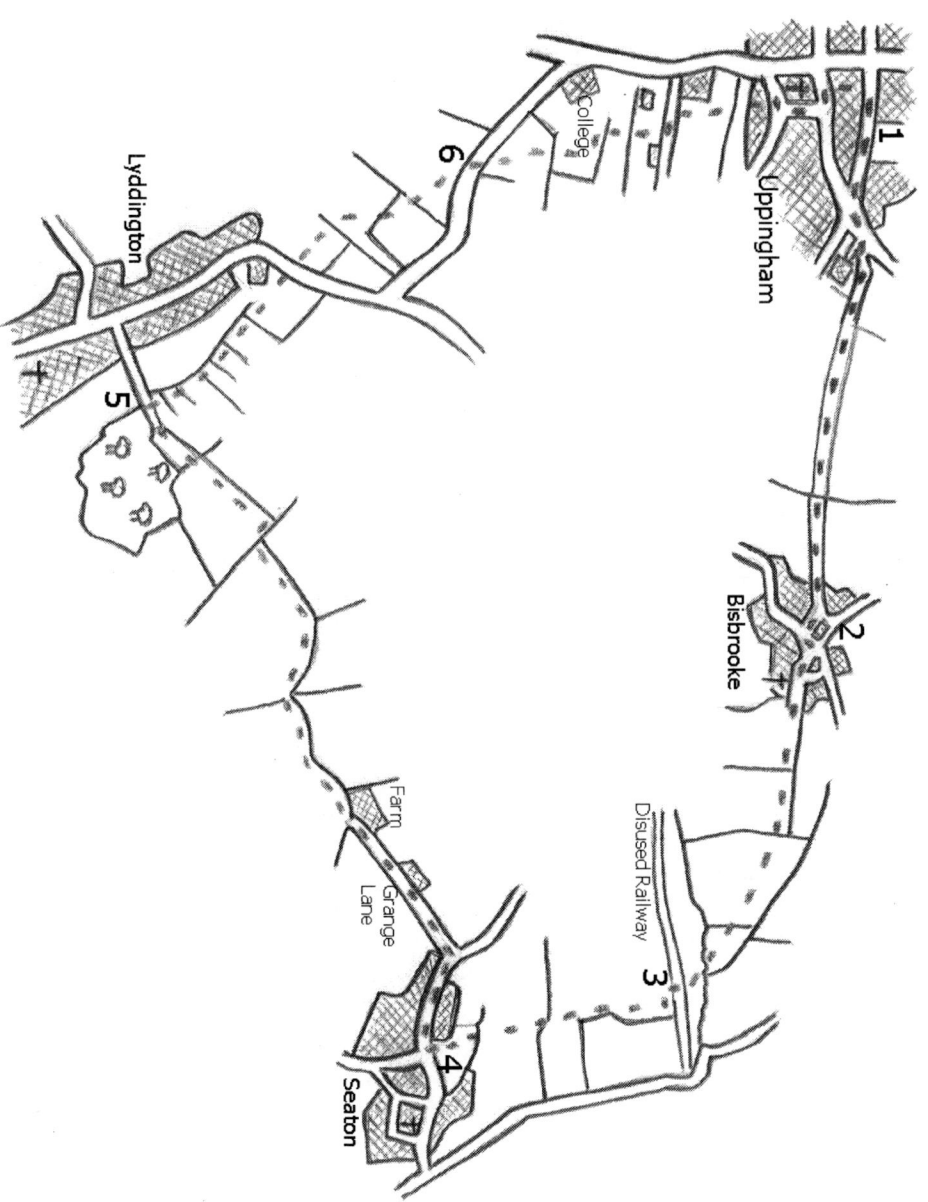

# 9  Allexton Park

## $7^1/_2$ Miles      $3^1/_2$ Hours

**Park in the lay-by** on the north side of the A47, 300yds east of the junction for Allexton and Belton in Rutland, at the bottom of Wardley Hill, 3 miles west of Uppingham. No toilets, caravan café open early morning to early afternoon, pubs in Belton.

**1** Facing the A47, turn right and walk along the verge to the adjacent junction, cross and go down the short piece of road into Allexton. At the corner of Main Street and Hallaton Road, carry straight on along Main Street; bear left then right just past the church. Go to the left at the T-junction; carry on as the lane ends in the signposted direction past the front of the house, along the overgrown path and over the stile.

**2** Walk diagonally right up the first part of the hill; turn right to follow the edge of the field with the fence to the right past the yellow topped marker post and through the gate. Maintain direction along this obvious farm track keep going as it bears right through the gap and over the stream joining Eye Brook. Go up to the A47, walk to the left hand end of the lay-by and cross this busy road.

**3** Go through the gate and cross the field; turn left with the hedge and Eye Brook to the right. Continue direction through several gates up to and past the farm and carry on through the small gate next to the larger gate on the right. Follow the left hand edge of this field to the corner and go through the gate. The path curves left around the end of an embankment where a railway bridge once stood to another gate. Go through and turn left to another gate, turn right along the right hand edge of this field and through gates either side of the next field and onto a road.

**4** Cross and walk down the left hand side of the field to the right. Go through the hedge gap and turn left by the marker post. Carry on through the gate and along the left hand side of this field to the road (the old A47).

**5** Turn left and walk through the village of East Norton. Turn right at the junction into Hallaton Road; continue over the A47 by-pass and through two gates on the old piece of road. Join the road ahead and take the field road to the left just before the road starts to go downhill, signposted Horninghold.

**6** Continue over a railway cutting/tunnel, for nearly a mile and follow the road right. Cross the stile and carry on, keeping fence and hedge to the left, past the Ordnance Survey triangulation pillar. Bear right at the marker post still with the hedge to left; go through the gate in the corner and down the enclosed track nearly to Fearn Farm.

**Completed on the next Page (Twenty Two)**

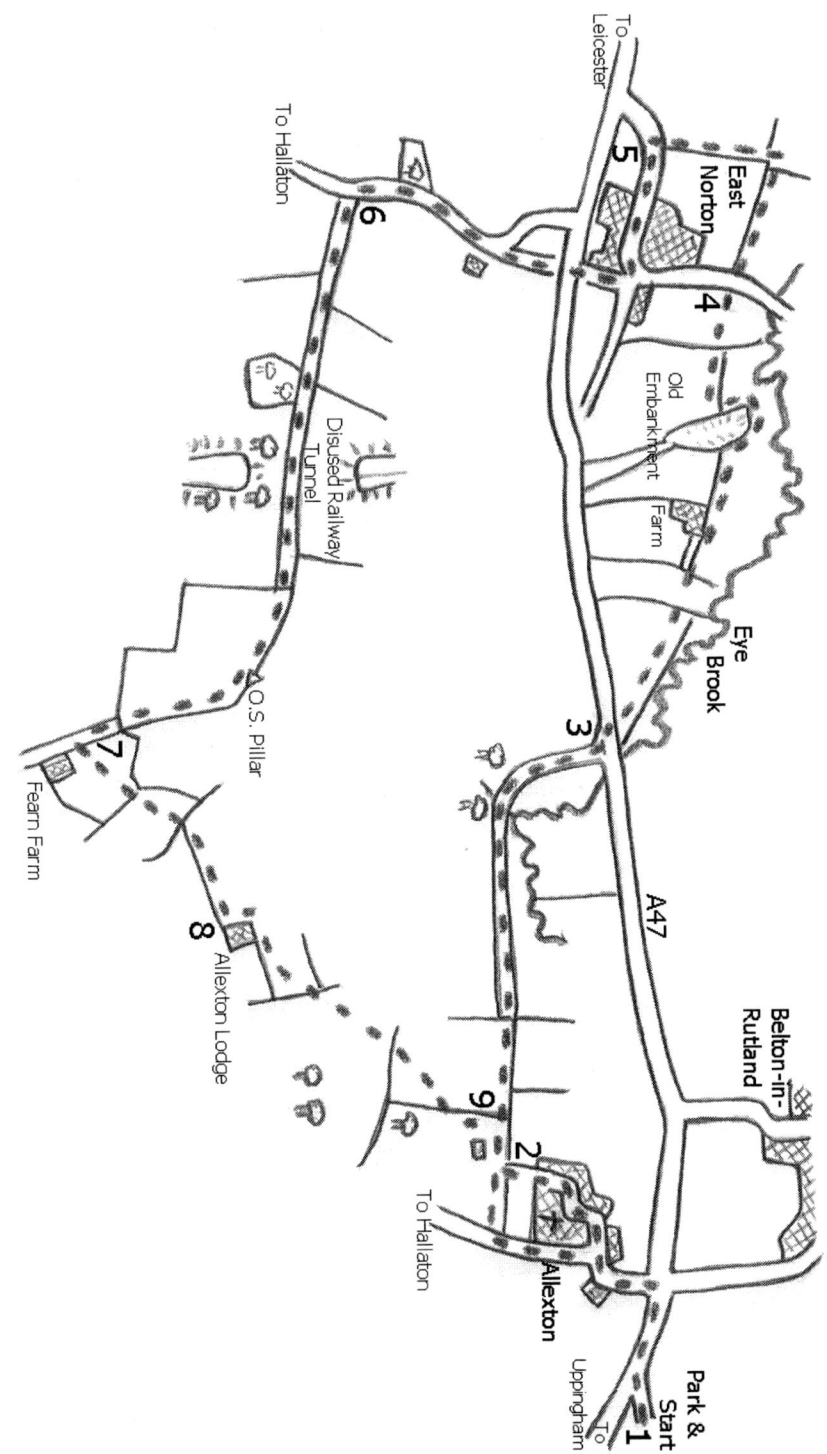

## Completion of 9 Allexton Park from the previous Page

**7** Turn left over the stile signposted Allexton, down the slope and through the gap next to the yellow top post. Take the upslope at a slight diagonal left; continue through the gate and on to the next marker post. Follow the field edge to the right keeping the hedge to the right.

**8** At the front of Allexton Lodge turn left, then right at the corner to regain direction, up to a marker post. Turn left here diagonally across the field (there may already be a track through the crop from the corner). Go through the hedge gap by the next marker post and turn sharper left on another diagonal, the track again should be visible, to the yellow top of a marker which should be in sight on the other side. Cross the stile/footbridge and maintain direction over this field. Cross this next stile and walk down the slope on the left of the field.

**9** Turn right on to the outward route but keep walking to the road with the hedge on the left. Turn left along the road to the A47 and bear right to the lay-by and your vehicle.

Also by Clive Brown:-

**'Easy Walking in South Bedfordshire and the North Chilterns'**

Published by the Book Castle @ £8-99
37 walks in your favourite style

9:G

## Hallaton Bottle Kicking  (See walks 1, 4 and 7)

Don't try to park in Hallaton to start any of these walks on an Easter Monday!  A quaint old English custom survives here.

On Easter Monday a contest takes place between the villages of Hallaton and Medbourne.  A Hare Pie is presented to the Rector for distribution to the crowd; the participants then form up into a procession, which led by a band, proceeds to Hare Pie Hill, where the competition takes place.

One of the bottles, which are actually purposely made small wooden barrels full of beer, is thrown to the crowd.  The intention is to place it over a defined boundary; there are few rules and even less of an attempt to enforce them, but the teams participate in a spirit of goodwill and friendly rivalry.

The winner is declared as the best of three; the victors return to the butter cross with the bottles and consume the beer inside.  The losers go back to the pub and consume the beer inside.

## Notes

# The 'Walking Close to' Series

## Peterborough
The Nene near Peterborough
The Nene Valley Railway near Wansford
The Nene near Oundle
The Torpel Way (Peterborough to Stamford)
The Great North Road near Stilton

## Cambridge
Grafham Water (Huntingdonshire)
The Great Ouse in Huntingdonshire
The Cam and the Granta near Cambridge
Newmarket

## Northamptonshire/Warwickshire
The Nene near Thrapston
The Nene near Wellingborough
The River Ise near Kettering
The Nene near Northampton
Pitsford Water
Rockingham Forest
Daventry and North West Northamptonshire
Rugby

## Leicestershire
Rutland Water
Eye Brook near Uppingham
The Soar near Leicester
Lutterworth
The Vale of Belvoir (North Leicestershire)
Melton Mowbray
The Welland near Market Harborough

## Lincolnshire
The Welland near Stamford
Bourne and the Deepings
South Lincolnshire

## Suffolk
Lavenham in Suffolk
Bury St Edmunds
The Stour near Sudbury
The Orwell near Ipswich
Dedham Vale
Stowmarket
Clare, Cavendish and Haverhill

## Berkshire
The River Pang (Reading/Newbury)

## Essex/Hertfordshire
Hertford and the Lee Valley
The Colne near Colchester
Epping Forest (North London)
Chelmsford

## Wiltshire/Bath
The Avon near Bath
Bradford-on-Avon
Corsham and Box
The Avon near Chippenham

## Bedfordshire/Milton Keynes
The Great Ouse near Bedford
The Great Ouse North of Milton Keynes
Woburn Abbey

## Somerset & Devon
Cheddar Gorge
Glastonbury and the City of Wells
The Quantock Hills
The East Devon Coast (Sidmouth, Branscombe and Beer)
Exmouth and East Devon

## Norfolk
The Norfolk Broads (Northern Area)
The Norfolk Broads (Southern Area)
The Great Ouse near King's Lynn
North West Norfolk (Hunstanton and Wells)
Thetford Forest
North Norfolk (Cromer and Sheringham)

## Nottinghamshire
Sherwood Forest
The Dukeries (Sherwood Forest)
The Trent near Nottingham

## Oxfordshire
The Thames near Oxford
The Cotswolds near Witney
The Vale of White Horse
Woodstock and Blenheim Palace
Henley-on-Thames
Banbury

## Cumbria
Cartmel and Southern Lakeland

## Hereford and Worcester
The Severn near Worcester
South West Herefordshire (Hay-on-Wye and Kington)
The Malvern Hills (2011)